BY THE SEA

Michelle Koch

Greenwillow Books
New York

Watercolor paints were used for the full-color art.
The text type is ITC Symbol Black.

First Edition   1 2 3 4 5 6 7 8 9 10

Library of Congress Cataloging-in-Publication Data

Koch, Michelle.
By the sea / by Michelle Koch.
p.   cm.
Summary: Labelled pairs of illustrations
introduce opposites found at the seashore.
ISBN 0-688-09549-6
ISBN 0-688-09550-X (lib. bdg.)
1. English language – Synonyms and antonyms –
Juvenile literature.   2. Seashore – Juvenile literature.
[1. English language –
Synonyms and antonyms.
2. Seashore.]   I. Title.
PE1591.K64   1991
428.1 – dc20   89-23344   CIP   AC

For Valerie
and Andy

near

far

throw

catch

foggy

clear

dry

wet

float

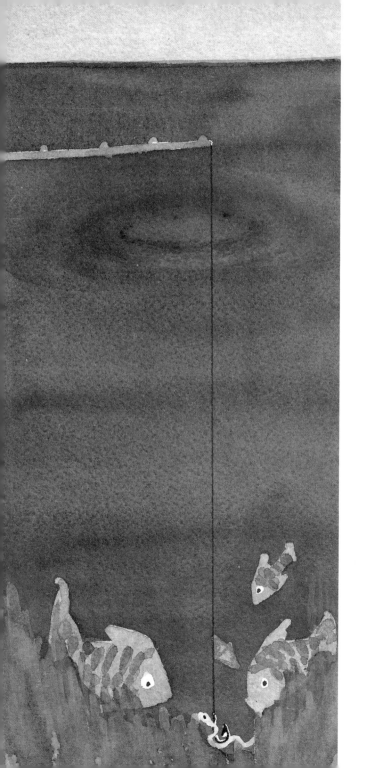

sink

deep

shallow

high tide

low tide

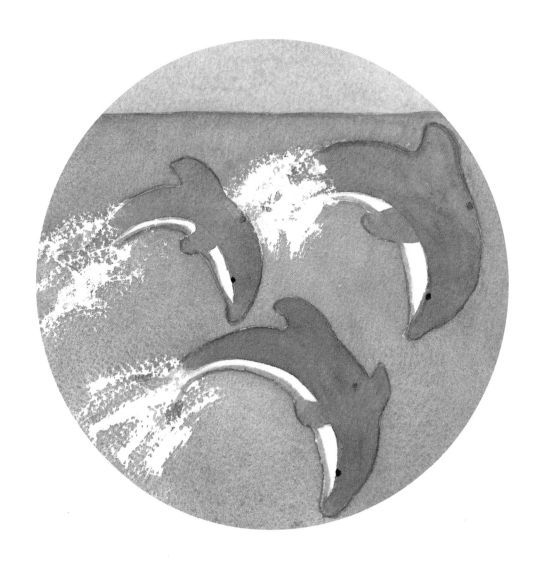

awake

asleep

empty

full

search

find